Unscripted:

Break Free From Societal Expectations, Creatively!

Tamera A. Khan

Text copyright © Tamera A. Khan 2025
Cover Design copyright © Tamera A. Khan 2025
All rights reserved.

Tamera A. Khan has asserted her right under the Copyright, Designs and Patents Act 1988 to be identified as the author of this work.

Although the author and publisher have made every effort to ensure that the information in this book was correct at the time of publication, the author and publisher do not assume and hereby disclaim any liability to any party for loss, damage or disruption caused by errors or omissions, whether such errors or omissions result from negligence, accident or any other cause.

This book has used AI-generated content, such as text, images or translations created by an AI-based tool.

No part of this book may be reprinted or reproduced or utilised in any form or by electronic, mechanical or any other means, now known or hereafter invented, including photocopying or recording, or in any information storage or retrieval system, without the permission in writing from the Publisher and Author. You must not circulate this book in any format.

First published 2025
by Rowanvale Books Ltd
The Gate
Keppoch Street
Roath
Cardiff
CF24 3JW

A CIP catalogue record for this book is available from the British Library.
Paperback ISBN: 978-1-83584-132-7
ePub ISBN: 978-1-83584-133-4

Contents

Disclaimer for Unscripted: Break Free from Societal Expectations, Creatively!.................... 7

Chapter 1: The Chaos of Being You 🌱🐚🦋............ 11

Chapter 2: Letting Go of Perfection 🪴..................... 24

Chapter 3: Living Outside the Lines 🖊..................... 37

Chapter 4: Choosing Your Own Path 🐾.................. 50

Chapter 5: The Power of Spontaneity ⚡................. 63

Chapter 6: Reconnecting with Your Inner Child 🐶..... 76

Chapter 7: Embracing Your Uniqueness 🌟............... 89

Chapter 8: The Art of Saying No ✋........................... 102

Chapter 9: Living with Imperfection 🌱..................... 113

Chapter 10: Cultivating Creativity 🐚......................... 126

Chapter 11: The Chaos of Change 🔄......................... 140

Chapter 12: Creating Your Own Rules 📝................. 153

Chapter 13: Finding Balance in Chaos 🌻................ 167

Chapter 14: Mindset Shift—Breaking Free from Limiting Beliefs 🔒................................. 181

Chapter 15: Defining Success for Yourself 🏆......... 197

Chapter 16: Taking Control of Your Life 🎮 212

Chapter 17: Embracing Failure & Learning 🚀 225

End of Book Message: Embrace Your
Unscripted Journey.. 240

Disclaimer for Unscripted: Break Free from Societal Expectations, Creatively!

1. Encouragement of Creative Freedom:

This book encourages you to express yourself creatively and embrace your authentic self. Explore the activities, prompts, and challenges in any way that feels right for you!

2. Respect Your Own Boundaries:

Always respect your personal boundaries when engaging in the exercises. If anything feels uncomfortable or overwhelming, take a step back and return to it when you're ready.

3. Respect Others' Boundaries:

While this book is about self-expression, we encourage you to respect others' boundaries. This journey is personal, and we support your freedom, but it's important to approach others with kindness and empathy.

4. Responsibility for Actions:

The activities in this book encourage personal expression, but your actions are your own responsibility. Please engage in them in a way that is safe and positive and in alignment with your values and comfort levels.

5. Respectful Creativity:

Use this book as a tool to express yourself creatively in a positive, uplifting way. We encourage free expression but ask that it be respectful of others and yourself. We do not condone violence, harm, or any form of negativity.

6. Mental Health Consideration:

If any activity or prompt causes distress, discomfort, or emotional challenges, we encourage you to take a break, reflect, or seek support. Your mental and emotional well-being should always come first. Creativity should empower, not overwhelm.

7. Encouraging Open-Mindedness:

Everyone's creative journey is unique! There are no right or wrong ways to interact with this book. Embrace the process, have fun with it, and enjoy the freedom of self-discovery without judgement.

8. No Violence or Harm:

This book celebrates creative freedom, but it does not support any form of violence, harm, or negative expression. Please use the prompts and activities in ways that foster positive, empowering energy.

9. Respectful of All:

We respect and celebrate diversity in all its forms. Whether you're working alone or with others, approach each activity with an open heart and an open mind, allowing others to express themselves in their own way.

10. Enjoy the Process:

This is your journey, and it's about having fun, being true to yourself, and breaking free from limitations. There's no rush—enjoy the ride, embrace the chaos, and discover how beautifully unpredictable life can be when you live Unscripted!

Unscripted: Break Free From Societal Expectations, Creatively!

Chapter 1:
The Chaos of Being You

Let's face it—life is messy. You are messy. And that's not a flaw; it's what makes you, you. From the moment we're born, society tries to put us into neat little boxes: act this way, dress that way, and follow these rules. It's exhausting, isn't it? Everywhere you turn, there's pressure to be someone else. Maybe it's social media influencers showing you a curated life that feels unattainable. Maybe it's family or friends subtly (or not so subtly) suggesting who you should be. But here's the truth: **there is no right way to be you—there's only your way.**

This chapter is about owning your chaos. Not fixing it. Not silencing it. But embracing every wild, wonderful, and unpredictable part of yourself. Think about it—some of the most brilliant, creative, and unforgettable people in history were the ones who refused to fit in. They were loud, different, and unafraid to take up space. And so are you.

So, let's stop apologizing for being too much or not enough. Let's stop filtering ourselves down to what's "acceptable". This is your permission slip to **be messy, be loud, be unapologetically YOU**. No edits. No script. Just pure, chaotic, authentic expression. Let's dive in.

Activity: *Scribble Out Your Identity*

Close your eyes and scribble wildly on the page for 30 seconds. Now, open your eyes and turn those scribbles into something—an animal, a face, a symbol of who you are. No erasing. No "fixing". Just embrace the randomness of YOU.

Challenge: *Tear, Smear, Crumple, Repeat!*

Rip this page out. Crumple it up. Unfold it. Smear some ink, coffee, or colour on it. Tape it back in. This is **you**—messy, chaotic, and still whole.

Writing Prompt: *The Beautiful Mess That Is Me*

Write the most **unfiltered, raw** description of yourself possible. Don't make it pretty. Make it real. Scribble, cross out, change direction mid-sentence. Let your words spill over into the margins. **What makes you, YOU?**

Activity: *The Unfinished Self-Portrait*

Draw yourself **without lifting your pen** off the page. One continuous, wobbly, imperfect line. No erasing, no overthinking. This is how your energy flows—without stopping.

Challenge: *Write in Every Direction*

Write about who you were **five years ago**, but here's the twist: write some words **upside down, sideways, backwards, in circles,** or in a shape. Let your thoughts **crash into each other** on the page.

Writing Prompt: *Your Thoughts on Shuffle*

Write **three random thoughts** that pop into your head right now, even if they make no sense. Then, connect them into a weird short story.

Activity: *Create a Controlled Explosion*

Take a page, splash colour on it (paint, markers, crayon, anything). Then, **fold** it in half while it's still wet. Open it. Your chaos just made art.

Challenge: *Do Something Wild*

Write down **one thing** you've always wanted to do but have been scared to. Now, **schedule it**. (Yes, really.) Even if it's small. Even if it's just a step toward it. Rip a piece of the page and carry it as a reminder.

Writing Prompt: *The Most Ridiculous Thing You Ever Did*

Write about a time when you **didn't** follow the rules. Maybe it was something small; maybe it was **chaotic genius**. What happened?

Activity: *The Sound of Your Chaos*

Turn on your favourite song. As it plays, **draw your feelings**. Fast, slow, sharp, wavy—it doesn't have to "be" anything. Just capture the energy.

Challenge: *Let a Stranger Decide*

Write down three random options (example: "Go outside and scream", "Write a poem with your non-dominant hand", "Rip out this page and throw it like confetti"). Ask a friend (or a stranger) to **pick one for you**. Do it. No second-guessing.

Writing Prompt: *Chaos Is My Superpower*

List **five things** that make you feel messy, unpredictable, or different. Now, write about how each one is actually a strength.

Chapter 2:
Letting Go of Perfection 🦋

Perfection is a myth. A soul-crushing, creativity-killing myth. Yet we chase it like it's the only way to be worthy. Maybe you've felt the pressure to get everything right—whether it's your grades, your career, your body, or your relationships. Maybe social media has convinced you that everyone else is effortlessly flawless, making you wonder why you're the only one struggling. Newsflash: **no one is perfect. Not even the people who seem like they have it all together.**

Let's be real: perfectionism is a trap. It tells you that if you can just fix this one thing—lose more weight, get a better job, have the perfect aesthetic—then, finally, you'll be happy. But the finish line keeps moving. And in the process, you lose sight of what actually matters.

This chapter is about **embracing imperfection**—because the things that make you different, quirky, and even flawed are what make you unforgettable. Let's stop waiting until we're "good enough" to show up in the world. Let's create, love, express, and take chances now, exactly as we are. The world needs real, not perfect.

Activity: *The Imperfect Doodle*

Close your eyes and draw something—anything. Keep your eyes shut the whole time. Open them and **admire the imperfection**. Label your masterpiece with a fancy title like it belongs in a museum.

Challenge: *Mess Up on Purpose*

Write a sentence with **at least five mistakes**. Spelling, grammar, backwards words—anything goes. Then, **decorate the mistakes**. Underline them, doodle on them, make them **beautiful**.

Writing Prompt: *The Time I Wasn't Perfect—And It Was Amazing*

Write about a time when something didn't go as planned… but ended up being way better because of it.

Activity: *Wreck This Portrait*

Draw a quick self-portrait. Now, **scribble over it, crumple the page, add wild colours, tear a corner**. You're still YOU, even when you're not "perfect".

Challenge: *Destroy the Rules*

Write down **three rules you've always followed** (example: "Stay inside the lines", "Be polite", "Always finish what you start"). Now, **break one right now**. Rip the page, colour outside the lines, write in messy handwriting—**let it go.**

Writing Prompt: *A Love Letter to My Flaws*

Write yourself a letter about everything "imperfect" about you—but **turn it into a love letter**.

Activity: *The Scribble Over*

Write a word or phrase you're afraid of (like "failure", "not good enough", "mistake"). Now, **scribble over it** until it disappears. Gone. No longer in control of you.

Challenge: *Mismatched & Beautiful*

Cut or tear out two random pieces from different pages. **Tape them together.** Now, turn it into something cool—a collage, a weird drawing, a random word mashup. Beauty doesn't have to match.

Writing Prompt: *The Most Glorious Mess I Ever Made*

Describe a time you **completely messed up**. What happened? What did you learn? Was it secretly kind of awesome?

Activity: *The One-Line Story*

Write an entire story in **one single, messy, run-on sentence**—no punctuation, no stopping, no worrying. **Just let it flow.**

Challenge: *Rip & Redesign*

Rip a piece of this page **without thinking**. Now, use the ripped piece to **create something new**. Draw around it, write inside it, fold it—**turn it into art**.

Writing Prompt: *What if Perfection Didn't Exist?*

Imagine a world where **"perfect" was never a concept**. What would life be like? How would people act? How would YOU feel?

Chapter 3:
Living Outside the Lines 🖊

Since childhood, we've been told to "colour inside the lines". Stay in your lane. Follow the rules. But who made these rules? And why do we blindly follow them? Think about it—everything in history that changed the world happened because someone dared to step outside the lines.

Maybe you feel stuck in a life that doesn't quite fit. Maybe you've been following a path that was chosen for you rather than one you actually want. It's time to break free. This chapter is about **daring to be different**—to question the rules, rewrite your own story, and create a life that feels like yours.

You don't need permission to live boldly. You don't need validation to follow your dreams. The only approval you need is your own. So, let's shake things up. Let's scribble all over the lines. Let's redefine what's possible. Your life isn't a template. It's a blank canvas. Paint it however you want.

Activity: *The Unpredictable Doodle*

Start a doodle in one corner of the page. Every **10 seconds, switch direction** without planning. Keep going until the entire page is full of unexpected twists and turns.

Challenge: *Write Upside Down*

Flip this book **upside down** and write a short sentence. It could be a thought, a dream, or a random phrase. Notice how weird and freeing it feels to do something in an unfamiliar way!

Writing Prompt: *If I Were Completely Free...*

Write about a day where you **had zero restrictions**—no schedules, no responsibilities, no rules. What would you do? Where would you go?

Activity: *The Forbidden Colour*

Choose a colour you **never** use (maybe one you dislike or never think to pick). Now, create an entire design, drawing, or pattern using **only that colour**. How does it feel to use something unexpected?

Challenge: *The Wrong-Hand Experiment*

Use your **non-dominant hand** (left if you're right-handed, right if you're left-handed) to write your name, draw something, or even attempt a signature. It's weird, right? But sometimes, the best things come from the unexpected!

Writing Prompt: *Dear Fear, You Don't Own Me*

Write a letter to something that has **held you back**—fear, doubt, hesitation. **Talk back to it.** Tell it why you're done letting it control you.

Activity: *The Line-Breaker*

Draw a **big, bold shape** in the middle of the page. Now, **ignore the shape** and write or draw straight across it— break the boundary!

Challenge: *Walk the Wild Path*

Trace your finger in random loops and swirls over the page, without lifting it. Now, use your design to create something—does it look like a map? A crazy new alphabet? A secret code?

Writing Prompt: *The Rule I Just Broke*

What's a **social rule or expectation** you've broken before? How did it feel? What did you learn?

Activity: *Erase the Expected*

Write a sentence about what people expect from you. Now, **erase words, scribble over them, cut them out, or replace them with new words** to create an entirely different meaning.

Challenge: *Cut & Rearrange*

Tear out or cut up a previous page (or an old magazine clipping), then **rearrange the pieces into something brand new**. A collage, a poem, a secret message—go wild!

Writing Prompt: *What if Life Had No Labels?*

Imagine a world where there were **no labels—no titles, no categories, no expectations**. What would change? How would people treat each other? How would YOU feel?

Chapter 4:
Choosing Your Own Path

There's a script society hands us: go to school, get a stable job, get married, have kids, retire. But what if that's not the story you want to tell? Too often, we follow paths because they feel safe, not because they make us happy.

Here's the thing—happiness isn't one-size-fits-all. Some people thrive in a traditional 9-to-5; others are meant to travel the world. Some want to build empires; others want a quiet, simple life. **There is no wrong way to live—only what feels right to you.**

This chapter is about giving yourself permission to take the road less travelled. To create your own definition of success. To stop living for expectations and start living for you. Because the life that makes sense to everyone else won't matter if it doesn't feel right to you. So, let's break the mould. Let's choose the path that feels exciting, even if it's unconventional. After all, the best stories are the ones no one saw coming.

Activity: *The Blank Map*

Draw a **winding path** across this page, with twists, turns, and crossroads. Now, **fill it with random words, symbols, or sketches** that represent your journey—challenges, dreams, surprises. **Where does your path lead?**

Challenge: *Detour Ahead!*

Pick a daily habit you follow **without thinking** (brushing your teeth, morning coffee, checking your phone). **Do it differently today.** Brush your teeth with the opposite hand. Take a new route to work. Skip the coffee and try tea. **See what happens when you change direction!**

Writing Prompt: *A Letter from Future You*

Imagine your future self—**5, 10, or 20 years from now**. Write a letter from them to you. What advice do they give? What do they want you to stop worrying about?

Activity: *Connect the Dots... Your Way!*

Draw **15 random dots** on this page. Now, **connect them** however you want—lines, zigzags, swirls, even a secret message. **No rules—just your own design!**

Challenge: *Say "No" (or "Yes") for a Day*

If you always say **yes** to things you don't want to do, **practise saying no** today. If you always hesitate, **challenge yourself to say yes** to something new. **See how it feels to choose for yourself!**

Writing Prompt: *Redefining Success*

Society says **success looks like X, Y, or Z**. But what does it actually mean to YOU? Write down **your own definition**—one that has nothing to do with money, status, or anyone else's opinion.

Activity: *Your Personal Motto*

Write down **three words or phrases** that define how you want to live. Make them bold. Make them messy. **Now, decorate the page like a personal banner!**

Challenge: *Unfollow the Noise*

For one hour (or a whole day), **stop scrolling**. No social media. No news. No outside input. **Just you, your thoughts, and whatever you feel like doing.** How does it feel to step away?

Writing Prompt: *The Road Not Taken*

Think of a time you **had to make a big choice**. What would've happened if you had chosen the other option? **Describe the alternate reality!** Would things be better, worse, or just different?

Activity: *The Wild Bucket List*

Forget the usual "travel the world" bucket list. **Write 10 things you'd love to do that seem weird, small, or totally YOU.** (Examples: start a food fight, wear pyjamas to the store, send a letter to a stranger.)

Challenge: *Ditch the Guidebook*

Choose **one thing** today—what you wear, what you eat, how you spend your time—**without** considering what's "normal" or expected. Just **do what feels right**.

Writing Prompt: *Who Would I Be if...*

Finish the sentence **as many times as you can**. *Who would I be if... I stopped caring what people thought? If I made decisions based on joy instead of fear? If I trusted myself more?*

Chapter 5:
The Power of Spontaneity

When was the last time you did something just because it felt right in the moment? Not because it was planned, not because it was "productive", but just because it made you feel *alive*?

We live in a world that glorifies structure, schedules, and carefully calculated decisions. But here's a secret: some of the best moments in life happen when you throw away the plan. Think about it—your most exciting memories, the ones that make you smile years later, probably weren't scripted. They were spontaneous.

But somewhere along the way, we're taught to fear the unknown. We're told to play it safe, to stick to routines, to overthink every decision. And in doing so, we trade adventure for predictability. This chapter is here to change that.

This is your reminder that **you don't have to plan everything**. You don't need to have all the answers before you take a step forward. Some of life's greatest experiences come from saying "yes" without overthinking it. So, let's practise the art of spontaneity—of taking risks, of following impulse, of embracing the thrill of the unknown. You never know what might happen when you stop planning and start *living*.

Activity: *Five-Minute Creative Frenzy*

Set a timer for **five minutes**. Now, **create something—ANYTHING**. A messy sketch, a wild poem, a random collage. No thinking, no judging—**just create until the timer stops!**

Challenge: *The Random Word Adventure* 📖

Ask someone for a **random word** (or flip to a random word in a book). Now, **use that word as inspiration** for something spontaneous—a doodle, a short story, or even a made-up song!

Writing Prompt: *The Alternate Reality Decision*

Think about a moment in your life when you had to make a choice. Now, **rewrite history**. What would have happened if you had chosen differently? **Write about this alternate version of your life!**

Activity: *Unplanned Scribble Art*

Without looking, **scribble all over this page** for 15 seconds. Now, step back and turn it into something—maybe a landscape, an animal, or a surreal design!

Challenge: *Reverse Your Routine*

Do something **completely opposite of your usual habits**. If you always listen to a certain genre of music, pick something entirely new. Brush your teeth with the opposite hand. **Shake up your routine and notice how it feels.**

Writing Prompt: *The Unexpected Visitor*

A **mysterious guest** arrives at your door—completely unannounced. Who are they? What do they want? **Write the story and let the plot unfold spontaneously!**

Unscripted: Break Free From Societal Expectations, Creatively!

Activity: *Dare Yourself—Literally*

Write **five fun dares** (nothing too crazy) on this page. Now, **pick one at random** and do it!

Challenge: *The 10-Second Outfit Switch*

Close your eyes, reach into your closet, and **put on the first thing you grab**—even if it makes no sense! Now, **wear it for an hour** and embrace the randomness.

Writing Prompt: *Write Without Stopping* 🖊

Set a timer for **three minutes** and just **write non-stop**. No erasing, no second-guessing. Let your mind spill out onto the page!

Activity: *Blindfolded Art*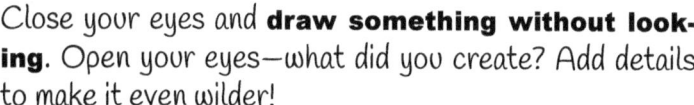

Close your eyes and **draw something without looking**. Open your eyes—what did you create? Add details to make it even wilder!

Challenge: *Spontaneous Compliment Challenge*

Find **three people** and give them each a **genuine, unplanned compliment**. Notice how it changes their mood (and yours).

Writing Prompt: *The Last-Minute Trip*

Imagine you have **one hour to pack and leave for a mystery trip**. Where are you going? What do you bring? **Write the adventure as if it's happening right now!**

Chapter 6:
Reconnecting with Your Inner Child 👶

When you were a kid, you didn't care about looking silly. You didn't hold yourself back from dancing, drawing, playing, or asking a million "why" questions. You were fearless, curious, and full of imagination. So, what happened?

Somewhere along the way, we're told to "grow up". We're taught that being playful is childish, that creativity is only for artists, and that we need to be serious to be successful. But growing up doesn't mean losing yourself—it means learning how to bring *every part of you* along for the ride.

This chapter is about **reclaiming that fearless, joyful version of yourself**. The one who didn't care what others thought. The one who dreamed big and believed anything was possible. You don't need permission to have fun, to create for the sake of creating, to enjoy life without constantly trying to be productive. Your inner child is still there—waiting for you to invite them back into your life.

Let's play again. Let's dream again. Let's live like we did before the world told us to be different.

Activity: *Doodle Like a Kid Again*

Grab some crayons, markers, or just a pen and **fill this page with doodles**. Stick figures, random squiggles, whatever comes to mind. **Draw like no one is watching.**

Challenge: *Write Your Name with Your Non-Dominant Hand*

Remember how hard it was to learn how to write? **Try it again!** Use your non-dominant hand and sign your name **like a five-year-old**. Embrace the wobbly letters!

Writing Prompt: *A Letter to Your Younger Self*

If you could talk to your childhood self, what would you say? **Give them advice, encouragement, or just tell them how awesome they are.**

Activity: *Make a Silly Face, Then Draw It*

Make the **silliest, most ridiculous** face you can in a mirror or a selfie. **Now, draw it!** Exaggerate everything!

Challenge: *Eat Like a Kid for One Day*

For one meal, eat something you loved as a child—maybe mac & cheese, candy, or cereal. **Enjoy it without guilt.**

Writing Prompt: *Your Funniest Childhood Memory*

What's a memory from childhood that still makes you laugh? **Write about it in all its chaotic, messy glory!**

Tamera A. Khan

Activity: *The Floor Is Lava!*

Pretend the floor is lava—**seriously**. Find a way to cross the room without touching the floor. **Bonus: draw your escape plan on this page!**

Challenge: *Sing Out Loud (Even Off-Key!)* 🎤

Sing your favourite childhood song as loud as possible. **No shame, just fun.**

Writing Prompt: *If You Could Be Any Kid Again...*

If you could relive **one day of your childhood**, which day would it be? **Describe it in detail**.

Activity: *Finger Painting Without Paint*

Use **your fingers to "paint"** with whatever you have—coffee, lipstick, dirt, or even just a dry pen. **Let go of precision and have fun!**

Challenge: *Build a Fort!* 🏰

Use blankets, pillows, and whatever you can find to **build a secret hideout**. Even if it's just in your mind, **draw a blueprint of your dream fort**!

Writing Prompt: *If Childhood You Met Adult You...*

Imagine meeting your younger self. **What would they think of you? What would they ask?** Write the conversation!

Chapter 7:
Embracing Your Uniqueness

The world tries to convince you that fitting in is the goal. That blending into the crowd is safer than standing out. But here's the truth: **the things that make you different are the things that make you unforgettable.**

Think about your favourite artists, musicians, or writers. The people who inspire you. They didn't become icons by being like everyone else. They became icons because they **owned** what made them different. And you can do the same.

Too often, we shrink ourselves to fit in. We edit parts of who we are, hoping to be accepted. But at what cost? When you hide your uniqueness, you dim your light. And the world doesn't need another copy—it needs you, in all your weird, wonderful, and wildly unique glory.

This chapter is about **celebrating what makes you stand out**. It's about unlearning the idea that different is wrong and embracing the fact that different is powerful. So, stop apologizing for being yourself. The people who matter will love you for it—and the ones who don't? They were never meant for your story anyway.

Activity: *Design Your Own Personal Logo*

If **you** were a brand, what would your logo look like? **Sketch it out!** Use symbols, colours, or even just a cool signature.

Challenge: *Wear the Boldest Thing You Own*

Dig into your closet and **put on something that makes you feel powerful**—even if it's weird, colourful, or totally mismatched. **Rock it for a day!**

Writing Prompt: *What Makes You... YOU?* ✎

List **10 things** that make you different from most people. They can be talents, habits, or even little quirks.

Activity: *Signature Pose Challenge* 📷

Come up with a **signature pose** that represents your energy. Draw it or take a photo. **Give it a name!**

Challenge: *Turn Your "Flaw" into an Advantage*

What's something about yourself that people have criticized? **Reframe it as a strength** and write about how it makes you unique.

Writing Prompt: *Your Unapologetic Manifesto* 📖

Write a **declaration of self-love**—a bold statement about **who you are and why you refuse to change for anyone**.

Activity: *Create Your Own "Weird" Holiday*

If there was a national holiday dedicated to you, what would it be called? **Describe how it would be celebrated!**

Challenge: *Do One Thing That Scares You*

Think of something you've always wanted to do but felt too afraid to try. **Do it today—or take the first step toward it!**

Writing Prompt: *Write a Love Letter to Your Quirks*

What's something weird or unusual about yourself that you love? **Write about why it's awesome.**

Activity: *Doodle Your Dream Self*

Draw yourself as the most **fearless, confident, and unapologetically YOU** version possible. **How do you look? What's different?**

Challenge: *Ask Someone What Makes You Unique*

Find a friend or family member and ask: **"What's something about me that stands out?"** Write down their answer.

Writing Prompt: If You Could Meet Your Future Self...

What would **future you** say to you right now? **Write their advice.**

Chapter 8:
The Art of Saying No

We've all been there—saying yes when we really wanted to say no. Agreeing to things out of guilt, obligation, or the fear of disappointing someone. But saying yes all the time comes at a price: your time, your energy, and your mental health.

The truth is, **saying no is one of the most powerful things you can do for yourself**. It's not selfish. It's not rude. It's setting boundaries, and boundaries protect your peace.

Social media and society make us feel like we need to be available all the time. If we don't say yes, we're missing out, letting someone down, or not doing enough. But real self-care isn't just bubble baths and deep breaths—it's knowing your limits and honouring them.

This chapter is about **owning your no**. Saying no to things that drain you. Saying no to people who take more than they give. Saying no to anything that doesn't align with what you want. Because every no you say to something that doesn't serve you is a YES to yourself.

Challenge: *Say NO Today—Guilt-Free!*

The next time someone asks for something that doesn't align with your energy, just say **No. No over-explaining. No apologizing. Just a firm, clear "No, that doesn't work for me".**

Writing Prompt: *What's Your Hardest "No" Yet?*

Write about a time when you struggled to say no. **How did it make you feel? How would you handle it differently now?**

Activity: *Redesign the "Stop" Sign* 🚦

What if a stop sign could reflect your personal boundaries? Draw your own version of a STOP sign that represents how you want to enforce limits in your life.

Challenge: *Cancel Something That Drains You*

Look at your calendar. Is there something you don't want to do but agreed to out of obligation? **Cancel it today. Feel the freedom.**

Writing Prompt: *Permission to Disappoint*

Write a letter to yourself, giving yourself permission to disappoint people who expect too much from you. **Because your peace matters more.**

Activity: *The "No" Art Page*

Use this page to scribble, tear, stamp, or collage a giant, unapologetic "NO". Decorate it however you like. Make it loud and bold.

Writing Prompt: *The "Future You" Boundary Letter*

Write a letter from your future, boundary-strong self. **What advice does future you have about protecting your energy and time?**

Activity: *Your "No" Mantra*

Create a mantra or affirmation that reminds you to stand firm in your decisions. **Example:** *"My time is valuable, and I choose where it goes."* **Write it, decorate it, and repeat it daily.**

Challenge: *Unapologetic Voice Memo*

Record yourself saying NO in different ways—firm, confident, direct. Play it back. Hear the **strength** in your own voice. **Own it.**

Writing Prompt: *If "No" Was Easy...*

What's something you wish you could say no to more easily? Write about why it's hard and how you can start setting that boundary today.

Chapter 9:
Living with Imperfection

We all have imperfections—parts of ourselves we wish were different, mistakes we wish we could undo, or struggles we'd rather hide. Maybe it's the way we look, the way we think, or the way we feel. Maybe it's a past failure or a habit we haven't quite broken yet. Whatever it is, we tend to view our imperfections as flaws that make us "less than" when, in reality, they are the very things that make us **real, unique, and human**.

This chapter is about **shifting your perspective**—about realizing that you are not broken, incomplete, or unworthy because of your imperfections. You are not meant to fit into some narrow, impossible definition of perfection that society has created. Instead of trying to erase or hide the messy, complicated, and flawed parts of yourself, **what if you embraced them?** What if you saw them as part of your story, part of what makes you strong, resilient, and beautifully one-of-a-kind?

Think about the people you admire most. Are they perfect? No. But what makes them inspiring is how they show up **despite their flaws, despite their struggles, despite their self-doubts**. True confidence doesn't come from pretending to be perfect—it comes from embracing who you are, imperfections and all.

So, let's stop striving for an **unattainable ideal** and start leaning into the truth: **you are perfectly imperfect, and that is more than enough.**

Your imperfections do not make you less. They make you real. They make you human. And they make you beautifully, uniquely you.

Activity: *Destroy This Page—Beautifully!*

Rip it, crumple it, scribble over it, spill something on it. Then turn it into a masterpiece. Messy art = real art.

Challenge: *Wear Your Flaws Proudly*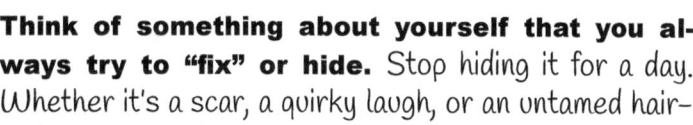

Think of something about yourself that you always try to "fix" or hide. Stop hiding it for a day. Whether it's a scar, a quirky laugh, or an untamed hairstyle—own it, celebrate it.

Writing Prompt: *The Beauty of a "Mistake"*

Write about a time when a mistake led to something amazing. Maybe you took a wrong turn and discovered your favourite café. Maybe a failed plan led to a better adventure. Imperfection creates magic.

Activity: *Imperfect Self-Portrait*

Draw a portrait of yourself without using an eraser. Don't try to make it perfect—just let the lines be as they are. Imperfect, but still you.

Challenge: *Post Something "Unpolished"* 📱

Share an unedited, raw moment—whether it's a photo, a doodle, or a thought—on social media or with a friend. **No filters. No overthinking. Just real.**

Writing Prompt: *Dear Past Me, You Were Already Enough*

Write a letter to your younger self, **telling them that they didn't need to be perfect. They were already worthy.**

Activity: *The Wabi-Sabi Hunt* 🔍

Wabi-Sabi is a Japanese philosophy that finds beauty in imperfection. Look around you—what's something that isn't "perfect" but is beautiful because of it? A chipped mug? An old book? A crooked smile? Sketch it or describe it here.

Challenge: *Do Something Badly—on Purpose*

Sing off-key, dance awkwardly, write a poem with terrible rhymes. **The goal? Feel the joy of doing something without pressure to be "good" at it.**

Writing Prompt: *The Perfectly Imperfect Day*

If you had a day where nothing had to be perfect—what would you do? No pressure to impress, no need to perform. Just being. Describe it.

Activity: *Unfinished Business*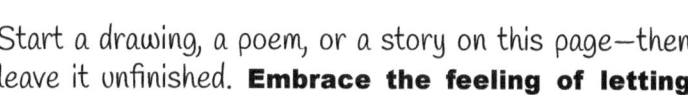

Start a drawing, a poem, or a story on this page—then leave it unfinished. **Embrace the feeling of letting something be incomplete.**

Challenge: *Say "I Don't Know"* 👻 ♀

Instead of pretending to have all the answers, admit when you don't know something. **Feel the freedom of not having to be perfect.**

Writing Prompt: *What's Your Favourite Imperfection?*

What's something "imperfect" about yourself that actually makes you uniquely you? **Write about it and why it matters.**

Chapter 10:
Cultivating Creativity

When people hear the word **"creativity"**, they often picture painters in front of a canvas, writers drafting their next novel, or musicians composing a song. But creativity isn't just for artists—it's for everyone. **Creativity is problem-solving. It's innovation. It's imagination.** It's the ability to take an idea and bring it to life, whether that's through **cooking, writing, designing, storytelling, dancing, or even organizing your space in a way that sparks joy**.

Think about the last time you found a clever way to fix something around the house, made up a bedtime story for a child, or brainstormed solutions to a challenge at work. That was creativity in action. The truth is, **creativity is not a talent reserved for a select few—it's a fundamental part of being human**.

This chapter is about **unleashing your creative potential** and breaking free from the idea that creativity is something you either "have" or "don't have". Creativity isn't about having **fancy supplies, expensive tools, or formal training**. It's about allowing yourself to **think differently, experiment fearlessly, and express yourself unapologetically**.

But here's something important to remember: **creativity is a muscle.** The more you use it, the stronger it gets. If you've ever felt creatively stuck or thought, "I'm just not a creative person", it's probably because you haven't exercised that muscle in a while—not because you lack creativity. Just like going to the gym strengthens your body, **engaging in creative activities strengthens**

your mind. And the best part? The more you create, the easier it becomes.

You don't have to wait for inspiration to strike. You don't have to be an expert. **Just start.** Doodle in a notebook. Try a new recipe. Write down a wild idea, even if it doesn't make sense yet. Dance in your room. Build something from scratch. Let yourself **play**. Creativity thrives when you allow yourself to **explore without judgement**.

The world doesn't need more people who suppress their ideas out of fear. It needs **your voice, your perspective, your vision**. Whether you share it with others or simply use it as a way to bring joy into your own life, **your creativity matters**. Keep creating. Keep experimenting. Keep dreaming.

Because the world needs **your ideas**.

Activity: *30-Second Doodle Storm*

Grab a pen and **doodle non-stop for 30 seconds**. No thinking. No planning. Just let your hand move. **Go!**

Challenge: *Create Something Out of "Nothing"*

Find an everyday object—like a paperclip, a sock, or a leaf. **Turn it into something new.** Give it a story, a purpose, or a personality. **No object is boring if you get creative with it.**

Writing Prompt: *If Creativity Had No Limits...*

If you could create **anything in the world**, without worrying about skill, money, or resources—**what would you make?** Describe it in vivid detail.

Activity: *Opposite Hand Art*

Draw or write **using your non-dominant hand**. It will feel weird. **That's the point.**

Challenge: *A Day Without Screens*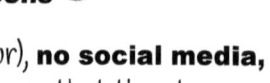

For one full day (or even just an hour), **no social media, no TV, no distractions**. Instead, use that time to **create**. Paint, write, build, craft—**whatever calls to you**.

Writing Prompt: *Reimagine a Classic*

Take a well-known story (Cinderella, Romeo & Juliet, etc.) and **rewrite it with a crazy twist**. Maybe Cinderella is a spy. Maybe Romeo & Juliet is set in space. **Make it wild.**

Activity: *The Soundtrack of Your Creativity* 🎵

Write down **five songs** that spark creativity for you. Now, **play one and create something while listening**. Let the music guide you.

Challenge: *The One-Line Story*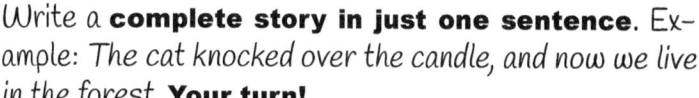

Write a **complete story in just one sentence**. Example: *The cat knocked over the candle, and now we live in the forest.* **Your turn!**

Writing Prompt: *Describe a Colour Without Using Its Name*

Pick a colour and **write a short piece about it—without saying what it is**. Describe how it feels, smells, sounds, or tastes.

Activity: *Creative Fusion*

Pick two random things from your surroundings and **combine them into a new invention**. Example: *a flashlight + a plant = a glow-in-the-dark tree!* Sketch it or describe it here.

Challenge: *Say Yes to Something Uncomfortable*
☑

Creativity thrives outside your comfort zone. Do **one thing today** that you normally wouldn't—something a little weird, unexpected, or new.

Writing Prompt: *Your Creative Manifesto*

Write a **pledge to your creativity**. What do you promise to do? **To create fearlessly? To experiment? To have fun?** Write it boldly.

Chapter 11: The Chaos of Change 🔄

Change is hard. Whether it's a small shift in routine or a life-altering transformation, stepping into the unknown can feel overwhelming, disorienting, and even terrifying. Our minds crave familiarity and predictability, so when change comes knocking—especially unexpectedly—it's natural to resist. But here's the truth: **change is inevitable, and more importantly, it's necessary.**

Think about the most meaningful moments in your life. Chances are, they didn't happen by staying in your comfort zone. They happened because something shifted. **Change is the spark that fuels growth, transformation, and new beginnings.** Without it, we remain stagnant, repeating the same patterns, stuck in the same cycles.

This chapter is about **embracing the chaos that comes with change** and finding the hidden opportunities within it. Instead of fearing change, what if we learned to welcome it? What if, instead of seeing it as something being taken from us, we viewed it as something making space for what's next?

Yes, change can feel uncomfortable. It can shake our sense of security and leave us questioning what's ahead. But discomfort is not a signal to turn back—it's a sign that growth is happening. **Real transformation doesn't happen when things stay the same. It happens when we are willing to step into the unknown, even when it feels scary.** 🚀

Activity: *Rip Up the Past* ✂

Write down something from your past that you're ready to **let go of**. Now, **rip the page up** into tiny pieces. (Burn it if you're feeling dramatic—but safely!)

Challenge: *Say YES to Something New*

Pick one thing today that you'd normally say "no" to—but **say YES instead**. Whether it's a new food, a new idea, or a new way of thinking, **lean into the unknown**.

Writing Prompt: *A Letter to Your Future Self*

Write a letter to yourself **one year from now**. What do you hope has changed? What do you want to remind yourself? **Seal it, and don't open it until next year.**

Activity: *The Spontaneous Switch-Up*

Switch up something **right now**. Change where you sit, change the hand you write with, change your name for the day. **Embrace the randomness.**

Challenge: *The 24-Hour Perspective Shift* 👀

For one day, **view everything as if you're experiencing it for the first time**. That street you walk down? **Really look at it.** That routine task? **Notice the details.** See how change **shifts your perspective**.

Writing Prompt: *Your Life, Rewritten* ✏️

If your life were a novel and this was the **plot twist moment**, what would happen next? **Write it like a story.**

Activity: *The What-If Game*

Write down five wild "What if?" questions. Example: what if I lived on a boat? What if I quit my job and travelled? Let your imagination **go wild**.

Challenge: *Do Something That Scares You (Just a Little)* 😨

Big or small, step into **something unfamiliar**. Maybe it's speaking up, trying a new hobby, or even just wearing an outfit you wouldn't normally pick. **Feel the change.**

Writing Prompt: *The Butterfly Effect*

Think of **one small decision** you made that changed your life in a big way. **Write about it.**

Activity: *Random Page Decision* 📖

Flip to a **random** page in this book and **do that activity**. No second-guessing! **Trust the chaos.**

Challenge: *Declutter One Thing* 🗑️

Change starts with **letting go**. Pick one thing—an old habit, a toxic mindset, or just a cluttered drawer—and **clear it out**.

Writing Prompt: *The Moment That Changed Everything* ⌛

Write about a moment in your life where **everything shifted**. Maybe you didn't notice it at the time, but looking back—you see it now.

Chapter 12:
Creating Your Own Rules

From the moment we're born, we are surrounded by **rules, expectations, and societal norms**—many of which we never even stop to question. We're told what success should look like, how we should behave, what paths we should follow, and even what dreams are considered "realistic". But here's a bold truth: **you don't have to follow those rules.**

This chapter is about **rewriting your own rulebook**—about stepping away from the invisible guidelines that dictate how you should live and instead, designing a life that aligns with your deepest values, passions, and desires. The beauty of life is that it's **not a one-size-fits-all experience**. Yet, so many of us feel pressured to fit into a mould that was never made for us in the first place.

Think about it—**who wrote the rules you're following?** Who decided that success means climbing the corporate ladder? Who said you need to get married by a certain age, own a home, or have a picture-perfect life to be considered "on track"? Many of the rules we live by weren't created by us, yet we **shape our lives around them** as if they are set in stone. **But what if they aren't?**

Imagine if you gave yourself permission to **question the rules** you've been following your whole life. What if you decided that instead of working a 9-to-5, you'd build your own business? Or instead of settling down in one place, you'd travel the world? Or instead of pursuing a career that looks good on paper, you'd chase a dream that truly excites you?

There is no universal definition of success, happiness, or fulfilment. **You get to define what those things mean to you.** And that means you also get to choose which rules to keep, which ones to break, and which ones to rewrite entirely.

Activity: *Tear Up the Rulebook*

On this page, **write down three "rules" you've been told to follow** (e.g., "You have to work 9–5" or "You should always be polite"). **Now, rip the page out and destroy it.** Burn it, shred it, crumple it—do whatever feels right.

Challenge: *Break a Small Rule (Safely!)*

Pick one tiny, harmless rule and **break it today**. Eat breakfast for dinner. Wear mismatched socks. Sit somewhere new. **Get comfortable with doing things your way.**

Writing Prompt: *Your Personal Manifesto*

Write your own set of **personal rules to live by**. Not society's. Not your parents'. **Yours.**

Activity: *Your Life, Your Design*

Draw or collage a **"perfect" day in YOUR world**. No limits. No rules. Just what feels right to you.

Challenge: *The 24-Hour Rebellion*

For one whole day, **question every rule you follow**. If you always do something a certain way, ask yourself, **"Do I actually want to do it this way?"** If not, change it.

Writing Prompt: *The Most Unapologetic Version of You*

Imagine yourself **living completely on your terms**. Describe what that looks like in vivid detail.

Activity: *Invent a New Tradition*

Create **a personal tradition** that means something to YOU. It could be **a solo celebration, a weird ritual, or a made-up holiday**. Now, **do it**.

Challenge: *Say NO to a Rule That Doesn't Work for You* ✗

Pick a rule or expectation you've been **pressured to follow but don't actually believe in**. Say NO to it today. **Own your decision.**

Writing Prompt: *Rewrite a Rule That Annoys You*

Pick a rule that you think is ridiculous or outdated. **Rewrite it in a way that makes sense for you.**

Activity: *Create Your Own Award* 🏆

Design an award for yourself based on **your own rules for success**. (e.g., "The Best at Being Themselves Award!") **Draw it, decorate it, and claim it.**

Challenge: *Do Something Completely Unexpected*

Shock yourself. Do something today that **no one (not even you) would expect**. Step out of the script.

Writing Prompt: *If Society Had No Rules...*

Describe a world where **there were no social rules or expectations**. What would be different? Would it be better? Worse?

Chapter 13:
Finding Balance in Chaos 🥀

Life can often feel like a **never-ending whirlwind**—a constant juggling act between work, relationships, responsibilities, and personal ambitions. The to-do lists never seem to end, and the pressure to keep up with everything can feel overwhelming. In a world that glorifies **hustle culture and productivity**, it's easy to fall into the trap of believing that **being busy equals being successful**. But here's the truth: **you don't have to do it all to live a fulfilling life.**

This chapter is about **finding peace and calm amidst the noise**—not by eliminating chaos altogether (because let's face it, life will always have its messy moments), but by learning how to navigate it with **grace, intention, and self-awareness**. It's about **embracing the unpredictability of life** while still creating space for mindfulness, relaxation, and clarity.

We often hear the phrase "work-life balance", as if there's a magical formula that allows us to distribute our time and energy evenly across all areas of life. But **balance isn't about having equal parts of everything—it's about knowing what matters most at any given moment**. Some days, your work might require more of your attention; other days, your family, your health, or your creativity might take priority. **And that's okay.**

Instead of striving for **a perfectly structured life**, what if we focused on **creating a life that feels good?** A life where we give ourselves permission to rest, to slow down, and to embrace the natural ebb and flow of things.

Go out there and **embrace the beautiful chaos of being YOU.** 🌟🫶🎉

Activity: *The Tornado of Thoughts*

Grab a pen and **write down every thought spinning in your head right now**. Don't organize them. Don't filter them. Just **let the storm out onto the page**. Now? **Turn that chaos into something beautiful.** Circle the words that stand out. Draw connections. Create a poem, a mind map, a wild scribble—**make art from the mess.**

Challenge: *Do the Opposite of Your First Instinct*

When life gets chaotic, we tend to react out of habit. **Not this time.** Pick one thing today where your instinct tells you to react a certain way—and do the opposite. See what happens.

Writing Prompt: *Describe Your Inner Chaos*

If the chaos in your mind had a shape, a colour, or a sound—what would it be? **Describe it in vivid detail.** Is it a roaring fire? A crashing wave? A swirling galaxy? Get deep with it.

Activity: *The Chaos Collage*

Use this page to create **a visual explosion of your life right now**. Rip up magazine clippings, doodle wildly, write random words—**turn this into a snapshot of your beautiful, chaotic energy**.

Activity: *The Balance Blueprint*

Use this page and divide it into four sections: **Mind, Body, Relationships, and Passion.** In each section, jot down activities, habits, or things that bring you a sense of balance in that area. Use colours, drawings, or symbols to make it visually engaging. This will be your personal **Balance Blueprint**—a reminder of what keeps you grounded amidst the chaos.

Challenge: *Let Go of Something That's Holding You Back*

What's one thing you've been clinging to—**an old idea, a past mistake, a "should" that no longer serves you?** Let it go. Rip up a piece of paper. Burn a note. Say goodbye to it in the mirror. **Release it.**

Writing Prompt: *Your Life's Chaos Symphony* 🎼

If your life was a song, how would it sound? **Would it be a wild drum solo, an unpredictable jazz improvisation, a soaring orchestra?** Describe it—or better yet, **write the lyrics to your personal chaos anthem**.

Activity: *Spin the Chaos Wheel*

Write down **six spontaneous actions** (e.g., "Draw a self-portrait with my eyes closed", "Dance for 30 seconds", "Write a note to my future self"). Close your eyes, spin your finger in a circle, and wherever you land—**do it!**

Challenge: *Find Stillness in the Madness*

Amidst the noise, the distractions, the responsibilities— **can you find a moment of pure stillness?** Take one full minute today to sit in the chaos **without reacting to it**. Just observe. Breathe. **Exist.**

Writing Prompt: *Chaos as a Superpower*

What if your chaos was your strength? **How does it fuel you? How has it shaped you into the person you are today?** Write about how your messiness, your unpredictability, your uniqueness **make you unstoppable**.

Activity: *Your Controlled Explosion*

Take a blank page. **Fill it with energy.** Scribble, paint, splash ink, rip edges, add colour, layer words—**create something that visually represents YOUR chaos**.

Challenge: *One Last Wild Act*

Do something completely unexpected. **Break a routine. Send a random message. Say something you've always wanted to say. Make a spontaneous decision.** The world is **yours to shake up**.

Writing Prompt: *Write Your Grand Finale*

If this book was a movie, **what would your final scene look like?** How would you end this chapter of your life? How would you celebrate your journey? **Write it. Make it epic.**

Chapter 14:
Mindset Shift—Breaking Free from Limiting Beliefs 🔒

Have you ever stopped yourself from trying something new because you thought, **"That's just not me"** or **"I'll never be good at that"**? Maybe you've avoided speaking up because a little voice in your head whispered, **"You're not smart enough"** or **"People will judge you"**.

Those voices? **They aren't real.** They are **limiting beliefs**—invisible walls you've built in your mind over time. And the wildest part? Most of them weren't even created by you.

From the moment we're born, we are taught **who we should be**. Parents, teachers, culture, social media—everyone has an opinion about what's "right" for us.

📌 *Be realistic.*

📌 *Stick to what you know.*

📌 *Some people are just born talented.*

📌 *That dream is too risky—be practical!*

Sound familiar?

Now, imagine if **some of the most iconic people in history had listened to those voices**.

🚀 **Albert Einstein** was told he'd never succeed because he struggled in school.

🚀 **J.K. Rowling** was told her book about a boy wizard was a waste of time.

🚀 **Oprah Winfrey** was told she wasn't fit for television.

🚀 **Michael Jordan** was cut from his high school basketball team.

If they had **accepted** those beliefs as truth, they would have never changed the world.

The truth is, **your beliefs shape your reality**. If you believe you're not good enough, you'll hold yourself back. If you believe you're capable, you'll keep pushing forward. **You have the power to rewrite your story.**

This chapter is about **breaking free from mental cages**. It's about **identifying the lies you've been told and replacing them with truth**. It's about realizing that **you are NOT stuck—you are limitless**.

By the time you're done here, you'll never look at failure, success, or **your own potential** the same way again.

Your mind is your greatest weapon—so make sure it's working FOR you, not against you.

Go ahead and name the following activities whatever you wish!

Activity: ✎

Write down three beliefs that you hold about yourself that have limited your growth. Be honest and specific about how these beliefs have held you back in different areas of your life.

Challenge: 🚀

Choose one of the limiting beliefs you identified and challenge it. Research or reflect on evidence that contradicts this belief. Write a list of examples or stories that prove this belief wrong.

Writing Prompt: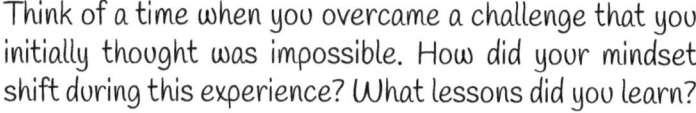

Think of a time when you overcame a challenge that you initially thought was impossible. How did your mindset shift during this experience? What lessons did you learn?

Activity: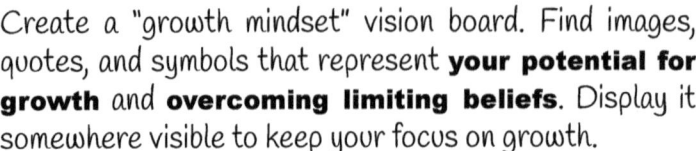

Create a "growth mindset" vision board. Find images, quotes, and symbols that represent **your potential for growth** and **overcoming limiting beliefs**. Display it somewhere visible to keep your focus on growth.

Challenge: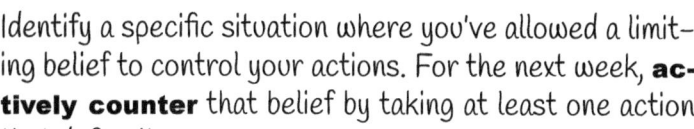

Identify a specific situation where you've allowed a limiting belief to control your actions. For the next week, **actively counter** that belief by taking at least one action that defies it.

Writing Prompt:

Write a letter to your future self, describing how your life will look after breaking free from your limiting beliefs. What will you be doing, and how will you feel?

Activity:

Practise affirmations for the next seven days. Choose three positive affirmations that directly counter your limiting beliefs. Write them down and say them out loud every morning.

Challenge: 🏆

Do something you've been avoiding because of a limiting belief. For example, if you think you're not good enough to speak publicly, find a small opportunity to speak up in a meeting or group.

Challenge: *The Rule Reversal Challenge*

Think of a "rule" or expectation you've been following without question—whether it's about your career, relationships, or personal life. Now, **flip the script**. For one day, challenge yourself to break that rule (in a positive way). For example, if you believe "rest equals laziness", intentionally take a break and enjoy it without guilt. Notice how it feels to **rewrite the rules on your own terms**. 🚀

Writing Prompt:

Reflect on a successful person you admire. Write about how their mindset might have influenced their success. What limiting beliefs do you think they had to overcome to reach their potential?

Activity: 🔍

Identify the source of one of your limiting beliefs. Was it something you were told by someone else, a past experience, or something you picked up over time? Write down how this belief was formed.

Challenge:

For the next 24 hours, actively **reframe** any negative thoughts that arise into positive, growth-oriented statements. Track your progress and journal how this changes your mindset.

Writing Prompt:

Write about a time when you successfully shifted your mindset in the face of adversity. What tools or strategies did you use to overcome the limiting belief at the time?

Activity:

Create a list of **new, empowering beliefs** that will support your growth and success. For each new belief, write one action step you can take this week to reinforce it in your life.

Chapter 15:
Defining Success for Yourself 🏆

What does it mean to be "successful"? **Money? Fame? A big house? A perfect life?**

For years, we've been spoon-fed **one narrow definition** of success. Society tells us that success looks like **a six-figure salary, a glamorous career, social status, and a picture-perfect life**.

But let's be honest—**how many people have all of that and still feel miserable?**

Social media is filled with people who seem to have "made it". They post luxury vacations, expensive cars, and highlight reels of their "perfect" lives. But here's what they don't show:

☹ **The exhaustion from keeping up an image.**

☹ **The pressure to constantly "outdo" themselves.**

☹ **The fear of losing it all.**

☹ **The realization that success doesn't always equal happiness.**

The biggest lie we've been told is that **success is a finish line**—something we "arrive" at. But success isn't a **destination**; it's a **direction**.

Let's switch the narrative. What if:

✅ Success meant **waking up excited about your day** instead of dreading it?

- ☑ Success meant **spending time doing what you love** instead of what society expects?

- ☑ Success meant **feeling deeply fulfilled**, whether that's from running a business, creating art, helping people, or travelling the world?

This chapter is about **giving yourself permission** to create a version of success that fits YOU. **Not your parents. Not society. Not Instagram. YOU.**

You were not born to live someone else's dream. Define your own success—and OWN IT.

Activity:

Write down your current definition of success. What does success look like to you right now? Reflect on how your definition has been shaped by external influences like society, family, or peers.

Challenge:

For the next week, challenge the traditional ideas of success that you see around you. Pay attention to media, social circles, or workplace expectations. **Reframe** them and ask yourself: *Does this align with my own definition?*

Writing Prompt:

Imagine a day in your ideal life. What does success feel like to you in this vision? Write about what you would do, who you would be with, and how you would feel. Don't hold back—dream big!

Activity:

Create a **Success Vision Board** based on your personal definition of success. Gather images, words, or quotes that reflect what success truly looks like for YOU—not what society or others think.

Challenge: 🗝️

Identify one area of your life where you're still holding on to an old definition of success that doesn't serve you. Take one **intentional action** today that moves you closer to your own vision of success in that area.

Writing Prompt:

Think of someone you admire who has defined success on their own terms. What about their life or achievements inspires you? How can you apply something from their approach to your own journey?

Activity:

Set a success goal for yourself that feels **authentically yours**. This goal should align with your core values and passions, not someone else's expectations. Write down clear steps to achieve it.

Challenge:

Over the next week, take one small step toward **living your own definition of success**. This could mean saying no to something that doesn't align with your values or taking time for self-care.

Writing Prompt:

Write a letter to your younger self, explaining how your definition of success has changed over time. What advice would you give them about staying true to their own vision, despite outside pressure?

Activity:

Reflect on how your **definition of success** is impacting your relationships and your community. How can you use your personal success to positively influence those around you? Write down your thoughts.

Challenge: 🔄

For the next 24 hours, **replace any thoughts of comparison** (to others or their success) with affirmations of **self-worth and progress** toward your own definition. Journal your experience afterward.

Writing Prompt:

Write about a time when you felt successful, even if it wasn't a traditional or external form of success. What made you feel successful in that moment, and why does that matter more than any external measure?

Activity: 🏆

List **five small wins** you've experienced recently that align with your personal definition of success. Celebrate them and commit to acknowledging similar successes going forward.

Chapter 16:
Taking Control of Your Life 🎮

Have you ever felt like life is just happening to you? Like you're stuck in a cycle of **doing what's expected**, but never what actually excites you?

🎮 **Go to school.**

🎮 **Get a degree.**

🎮 **Get a "stable" job.**

🎮 **Follow the rules.**

🎮 **Work hard, retire, then maybe start living.**

But what if this **default path** isn't meant for you? What if you were meant to take **a completely different route**—one that lights you up inside?

The world is filled with **people who played by the rules and still ended up unhappy**. They did everything "right" but still feel lost. Why? **Because they let life control them instead of taking control of life.**

Here's a truth bomb:

🎮 **No one is going to hand you your dream life. You have to create it.**

This chapter is about **breaking free from autopilot**. It's about:

♦ **Setting boundaries**—so people stop deciding your life for you.

♦ **Making bold choices**—even when they scare you.

♦ **Saying NO to things that drain you.**

♦ **Saying YES to opportunities that excite you.**

Imagine if, years from now, you looked back at your life and realized you never took control. Would you be okay with that? If the answer is no, **this is your wake-up call**.

Your life is your own. Take the damn wheel.

Activity: 🔍

Identify one area of your life where you feel out of control. Write down what specifically makes you feel this way and brainstorm three things you *can* control within that situation.

Challenge:

For the next seven days, commit to making one small decision each day that puts you in control—whether it's setting boundaries, making a proactive choice, or taking action toward a goal.

Writing Prompt:

Reflect on a time when you felt truly in control of your life. What was different about that period? What mindset, habits, or actions contributed to your sense of control?

Activity: 🎯

Write down five things in your life that you can control and five things that are out of your control. Focus on taking action on the things you can influence, and practise letting go of what you can't.

Challenge:

Say **"no"** to something that drains your energy or doesn't align with your priorities. Whether it's an unnecessary obligation, toxic relationship, or self-doubt, take action to remove it from your life.

Writing Prompt:

Write a letter to your future self, describing how your life has transformed now that you've taken full control of your decisions, mindset, and actions. Be as detailed and inspiring as possible!

Activity:

Write one word that describes yourself and fill this page with that word. Use different colours. Try writing in different fonts. Write sideways. Write upside down. Write big. Write small. Be authentically yourself.

Activity: 🛠

Write a **"Personal Power Plan"**. Outline three areas of your life where you want more control, the biggest obstacles in your way, and one actionable step you'll take for each.

Challenge: 17

Take control of your schedule! Plan your day *intentionally*, setting aside time for things that matter to you (self-care, growth, relationships) instead of letting your time be dictated by others.

Writing Prompt:

If you had **unlimited confidence and resources**, what would you take control of in your life right now? Write about the first steps you'd take and how it would change your life.

Activity:

Write down three **empowering affirmations** that remind you that you are in control of your life. Repeat them daily for the next week to reinforce your mindset shift.

Chapter 17:
Embracing Failure & Learning 🚀

Let's get one thing straight—**failure is not the enemy.**

But most of us treat it like it is. **We're terrified of messing up, of being judged, of falling short.** We're conditioned to believe that **failing = not good enough**.

✘ **Bombed a test? You're not smart enough.**

✘ **Business idea flopped? You're not cut out for success.**

✘ **Got rejected? You're not worthy.**

But here's what no one tells you: **every time you fail, you're getting closer to success.**

📌 **Steven Spielberg was rejected from film school three times.**

📌 **Thomas Edison failed 1,000 times before inventing the light bulb.**

Failure doesn't mean you're not good enough. **It means you're trying.** It means you're learning. It means you're moving forward.

This chapter is about **rewiring your relationship with failure**. Instead of running from it, you'll learn to:

◆ **Use failure as a stepping stone.**

◆ **See mistakes as lessons, not setbacks.**

◆ **Build resilience and keep pushing forward.**

Because in the end, success isn't about never failing. It's about **failing, learning, adapting, and trying again**.

You don't lose when you fail. You lose when you give up.

Activity: "Failure Resume"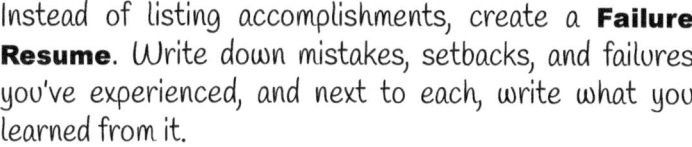

Instead of listing accomplishments, create a **Failure Resume**. Write down mistakes, setbacks, and failures you've experienced, and next to each, write what you learned from it.

Challenge: *"Fail on Purpose"*

For one day, **intentionally do something you might fail at**. Whether it's trying a new skill, speaking up in a meeting, or pitching an idea, embrace the discomfort and reflect on the experience.

**Writing Prompt: *"If I Knew I Couldn't Fail..."* **

What would you do if **failure wasn't an option**? Write about the risks you'd take, the dreams you'd chase, and what's stopping you from trying anyway.

Activity: *"Reframe a Past Failure"*

Take a **specific failure** from your past and rewrite it as a **lesson learned**. Instead of, "I failed at this", write, "This experience taught me..."

Challenge: *"The Three-Day Bounce Back"* 💀 ♂

Choose a failure that still stings. Over the next three days, take **one small action each day** to move forward. Whether it's learning from it, adjusting your strategy, or trying again, commit to bouncing back.

Writing Prompt: *"The Best Failure of My Life"*

Think of a **failure that turned out to be a blessing in disguise**. Write a short story about how it led to unexpected growth or opportunity.

Activity: *"Success Stories of Failure"*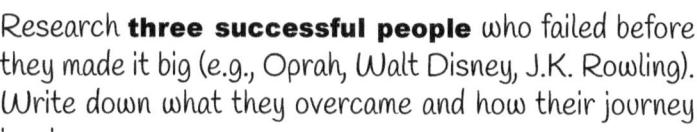

Research **three successful people** who failed before they made it big (e.g., Oprah, Walt Disney, J.K. Rowling). Write down what they overcame and how their journey inspires you.

Challenge: *"Tell Someone About a Failure"*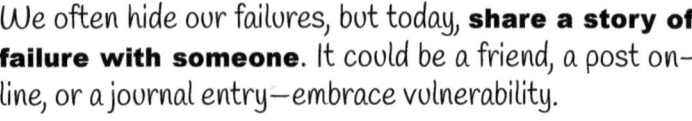

We often hide our failures, but today, **share a story of failure with someone**. It could be a friend, a post online, or a journal entry—embrace vulnerability.

Writing Prompt: "A Letter to My Younger Self About Failure"

Write a letter to your younger self, reassuring them that failure isn't the end—it's a stepping stone. Share wisdom and advice you've learned along the way.

Activity: *"The Five Whys"*

Take a **recent failure** and ask yourself **"Why?"** five times. Dig deep into the root cause of the setback, and identify how you can improve moving forward.

Challenge: *"Redefine Success & Failure"*

Write your **own new definitions** for *success* and *failure*. What does success look like to YOU? How can failure be **a part of success** rather than the opposite of it?

Writing Prompt: *"My Fear of Failing List"*

Write down **three things you're afraid to fail at**. Next to each, write what's the **worst that could happen** and what you'd do if it did. Is it as bad as you thought?

Activity: *"Celebrate a Failure"*

Pick a past failure and **celebrate it**. Treat it like a milestone, because it brought you **growth, experience, and wisdom**. Do something small to honour how far you've come!

End of Book Message:
Embrace Your Unscripted Journey

Congratulations on reaching the end of this book—but more importantly, the **beginning of a new chapter in your life**.

By now, you've explored the power of **mindset shifts, defining success on your own terms, taking control of your life, and embracing failure as a stepping stone**. You've challenged limiting beliefs, stepped outside of societal expectations, and hopefully discovered a deeper sense of who you are and what you truly want.

But remember, **this is just the start**. Transformation doesn't happen overnight, and there will still be moments of doubt, setbacks, and challenges. The difference now is that you have the **tools, awareness, and confidence** to keep moving forward—on your own terms.

This journey isn't about perfection. It's about **growth**. It's about **courage**. It's about having the audacity to create a life that feels authentic, fulfilling, and aligned with your purpose. **Your story is still being written, and you hold the pen.**

As the saying goes, **"The journey of a thousand miles begins with a single step"**. Keep taking those steps, no matter how small, because **consistency is key**. Every choice you make, every belief you shift, and every action you take brings you closer to the life you envision.

Final Challenge: take one insight, lesson, or action from this book and apply it within the next 24 hours. Small steps lead to big transformations.

Thank you for allowing me to be a part of your journey. I can't wait to see where your **unscripted** path takes you. 🚀

With gratitude and belief in your limitless potential,
Tamera

Author Profile

Tamera, known as the **Grandmaster of Creativity**, is a Caribbean-based author with a passion for **creativity, authenticity, and personal transformation**. Having studied at **Yale, the University of London, the State University of New York, Johns Hopkins University, and the University of California**, she blends academic insight with a deep curiosity about the **human mind, body, and spirit**. Tamera's mission is to **inspire others to break free from societal expectations and embrace their true creativity and authenticity**. She believes that **true freedom comes from self-expression and rejecting limiting norms**. Through her books and creative work, she encourages people to **challenge convention, think outside the box, and rediscover their inner voice**. She enjoys exploring different artistic mediums and is always on the lookout for **unconventional ways to spark creativity**. With exciting new books, projects, and creative initiatives on the horizon, she is dedicated to **making a lasting impact**. A natural **rebel** when it comes to traditional thinking, Tamera thrives on discovering **new and unconventional ways to inspire change through creativity and writing. Fun fact:** she believes **creativity isn't just an outlet—it's a way of life**.

What Did You Think of
Unscripted: Break Free from Societal Expectations, Creatively?

A big thank you for purchasing this book. It means a lot that you chose this book specifically from such a wide range on offer. I do hope you enjoyed it.

Book reviews are incredibly important for an author. All feedback helps them improve their writing for future projects and for developing this edition. If you are able to spare a few minutes to post a review on Amazon, that would be much appreciated.

Publisher Information

Rowanvale Books provides publishing services to independent authors, writers and poets all over the globe. We deliver a personal, honest and efficient service that allows authors to see their work published, while remaining in control of the process and retaining their creativity. By making publishing services available to authors in a cost-effective and ethical way, we at Rowanvale Books hope to ensure that the local, national and international community benefits from a steady stream of good quality literature.

For more information about us, our authors or our publications, please get in touch.

www.rowanvalebooks.com
info@rowanvalebooks.com

www.ingramcontent.com/pod-product-compliance
Lightning Source LLC
Chambersburg PA
CBHW050029090426
42735CB00021B/3423